Folk Music

North American Folklore

Children's Folklore

Christmas and Santa Claus Folklore

Contemporary Folklore

Ethnic Folklore

Family Folklore

Firefighters' Folklore

Folk Arts and Crafts

Folk Customs

Folk Dance

Folk Fashion

Folk Festivals

Folk Games

Folk Medicine

Folk Music

Folk Proverbs and Riddles

Folk Religion

Folk Songs

Folk Speech

Folk Tales and Legends

Food Folklore

Regional Folklore

North American Folklore

Folk Music

BY PETER SIELING

Mason Crest Publishers

Mason Crest Publishers Inc.
370 Reed Road
Broomall, Pennsylvania 19008
(866) MCP-BOOK (toll free)
www.masoncrest.com

First printing
1 2 3 4 5 6 7 8 9 10
Library of Congress Cataloging-in-Publication Data on file at the Library of Congress.
ISBN 1-59084-342-8
        1-59084-328-2 (series)

Design by Lori Holland.
Composition by Bytheway Publishing Services, Binghamton, New York.
Cover design by Joe Gilmore.
Printed and bound in the Hashemite Kingdom of Jordan.

Picture credits:
Corbis: pp. 66, 68, 96
Corel: pp. 11, 15, 18, 22, 23, 24, 29, 32, 42, 46, 47, 58, 80, 82, 90
J. Rowe: p. 71
PhotoDisc: pp. 8, 14, 20, 60, 72, 92
Cover: "The Organist" by Norman Rockwell © SEPS: Licensed by Curtis Publishing, Indianapolis, IN. www.curtispublishing.com

Printed by permission of the Norman Rockwell Family
© the Norman Rockwell Family Entities

Contents

Folklore grows from long-ago
seeds. Just as an acorn sends
down roots even as it shoots up
leaves across the sky, folklore is
rooted deeply in the past and
yet still lives and grows today.
It spreads through our modern
world with branches as wide
and sturdy as any oak's;
it grounds us in yesterday even
as it helps us make sense of
both the present and the future.

Introduction

by Dr. Alan Jabbour

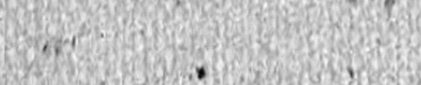

WHAT DO A TALE, a joke, a fiddle tune, a quilt, a jig, a game of jacks, a saint's day procession, a snake fence, and a Halloween costume have in common? Not much, at first glance, but all these forms of human creativity are part of a zone of our cultural life and experience that we sometimes call "folklore."

The word "folklore" means the cultural traditions that are learned and passed along by ordinary people as part of the fabric of their lives and culture. Folklore may be passed along in verbal form, like the urban legend that we hear about from friends who assure us that it really happened to a friend of their cousin. Or it may be tunes or dance steps we pick up on the block, or ways of shaping things to use or admire out of materials readily available to us, like that quilt our aunt made. Often we acquire folklore without even fully realizing where or how we learned it.

Though we might imagine that the word "folklore" refers to cultural traditions from far away or long ago, we actually use and enjoy folklore as part of our own daily lives. It is often ordinary, yet we often remember and prize it because it seems somehow very special. Folklore is culture we share with others in our communities, and we build our identities through the sharing. Our first shared identity is family identity, and family folklore such as shared meals or prayers or songs helps us develop a sense of belonging. But as we grow older we learn to belong to other groups as well. Our identities may be ethnic, religious, occupational, or regional—or all of these, since no one has only one cultural identity. But in every case, the identity is anchored and strengthened by a variety of cultural traditions in which we participate and share with our neighbors. We feel the threads of connection with people we know, but the threads extend far beyond our own immediate communities. In a real sense, they connect us in one way or another to the world.

Folklore possesses features by which we distinguish ourselves from each other. A certain dance step may be African American, or a certain story urban, or a certain hymn Protestant, or a certain food preparation Cajun. Folklore can distinguish us, but at the same time it is one of the best ways we introduce ourselves to each other. We learn about new ethnic groups on the North American landscape by sampling their cuisine, and we enthusiastically adopt musical ideas from other communities. Stories, songs, and visual designs move from group to group, enriching all people in the process. Folklore thus is both a sign of identity, experienced as a special marker of our special groups, and at the same time a cultural coin that is well spent by sharing with others beyond our group boundaries.

Folklore is usually learned informally. Somebody, somewhere, taught us that jump rope rhyme we know, but we may have trouble remembering just where we got it, and it probably wasn't in a book that was assigned as homework. Our world has a domain of formal knowledge, but folklore is a domain of knowledge and culture that is learned by sharing and imitation rather than formal instruction. We can study it formally—that's what we are doing now!—but its natural arena is in the informal, person-to-person fabric of our lives.

Not all culture is folklore. Classical music, art sculpture, or great novels are forms of high art that may contain folklore but are not themselves folklore. Popular music or art may be built on folklore themes and traditions, but it addresses a much wider and more diverse audience than folk music or folk art. But even in the world of popular and mass culture, folklore keeps popping up around the margins. E-mail is not folklore—but an e-mail smile is. And college football is not folklore—but the wave we do at the stadium is.

This series of volumes explores the many faces of folklore throughout the North American continent. By illuminating the many aspects of folklore in our lives, we hope to help readers of the series to appreciate more fully the richness of the cultural fabric they either possess already or can easily encounter as they interact with their North American neighbors.

Some of the earliest folk musicians used two wooden spoons for percussion.

ONE

What Is Folk Music?
A Definition

If you take music lessons, you may know a good deal of folk music without even realizing it.

L'M SURE YOU know the tune to the "Battle Hymn of the Republic." The last time you sang the familiar melody, by any chance did you use these words?

> *Glory, glory Hallelujah,*
> *Teacher hit me with a ruler.*
> *Hit her on the bean with a rotten tangerine*
> *And the teacher don't teach no more.*
> (traditional school folk song)

What do you mean I got the words wrong? How do you sing it? All I can say is my version is probably closer to the original than yours, because I'm a lot older than you!

How about this version of the same tune:

> *I wear my pink pajamas in the summer when it's hot*
> *I wear my flannel nightie in the winter when it's not.*
> *And sometimes in the springtime*
> *And sometimes in the fall*
> *I jump between the sheets with*
> *NOTHING ON AT ALL!*
> (Boy Scout song)

Did you ever sing this around the campfire on a scout outing? You may have—but I doubt Julia Ward Howe (1819–1910) would have liked those verses at all.

Julia Ward Howe was the editor of an **abolitionist** paper and champion of women's *suffrage* and other reform movements. One night, when she was visiting Northern Civil War troops at their camp, she heard the soldiers around their campfire singing these words to that same familiar tune:

> *John Brown's body lies a-mouldering in the grave,*
> *John Brown's body lies a-mouldering in the grave,*
> *John Brown's body lies a-mouldering in the grave,*
> > *His truth is marching on.*

Howe didn't care for those words either. A friend remarked to her that such a great tune ought to have more inspiring lyrics. Couldn't Julia, a writer and poet, come up with something? Unable to sleep that night (maybe because of all the bugs and mosquitoes), Mrs. Howe got up and penned the now famous words:

> *Mine eyes have seen the glory of the coming of the Lord,*
> > *He is trampling out the vintage where the*
> > *grapes of wrath are stored:*
> *He hath loosed the fateful lightning of His terrible swift sword—*
> > *His truth is marching on.*

The Union chaplain taught the words to the troops—and a tune that had been a folk tradition became a hit with a new set of lyrics. But at this point, should we still classify the "Battle Hymn of the Republic" as folk music?

That's a difficult question to answer. Folk music is hard to define. Like the trumpet of a wild bull elephant, you recognize it when you see or hear it, but it is not easy to describe in print. Every time you try to pin down a good definition, folk music slithers out of your grip and you find an exception.

Folk music is sometimes defined as music with an unknown

Folk songs are often sung around the campfire.

composer. We know the composer of the "Battle Hymn of the Republic"'s words but not the tune. Sometimes the melody's composer is known and the words are not. Sometimes unknown authors are discovered. If someday I am rummaging thorough old medieval manuscripts in a crumbling castle and I find this:

> *This is to certify that I, Erasemuch of Muckshire, hath written a new tune I hearby entitle: "Battle Hymn of the Republick" and do hereby register at the copyright office at Camelot. . .*

I may have discovered the author of the melody, but that doesn't usually remove a song from the category of "folk music." Some of our most beloved folk music has had well-known authors. For example, "Oh Susanna" and "Way Down upon the Swanee River" by Stephen Foster are considered folk music by most people.

One characteristic of folk music is that it is passed from one generation to the next by word of mouth, a chain of musicians passing along a tune without benefit of written notes. Each singer or musician hears it from someone else—and each musician tends to change the song to varying degrees. This results in wide variations in the tune, the words, or both. Few folk musicians read music but rather play or sing by ear.

Once folk music is written or recorded, however, it doesn't cease to be folk music. The "Battle Hymn" is a good example. It has a tune of unknown origin, perhaps one of the catchiest ever composed. Someone put some words to it and turned it into a popular sing-around-the-campfire song. A real poet got hold of it and turned it into a song that you'll find in practically every song collection ever written. And then countless generations of children used it to carry various rebellious or amusingly disrespectful sentiments. The tune is now a part of the collective American consciousness.

Folk music that is not written can become extinct in one generation. Fortunately, some people collect songs and write them down. Just as soon as people learned how to record music, they began rooting through the hills and countryside looking for folk musicians and recording them. People like Alan Lomax have preserved this musical heritage for us all. Old recordings of folk music may sound crude in comparison with modern professional musicians, but they have an energy and style that creates a different kind of beauty from the polished, professional version.

Original folk music is often rustic and unpolished sounding, performed by ordinary people rather than professional musicians. It might be functional in nature. For instance, the old African American work songs brightened up backbreaking labor, providing a rhythm for the work. Hymns and spirituals are sung to point worshipers' hearts toward God. Folk music is also pure enter-

> Alan Lomax and his father John Lomax were both important collectors of American folk songs. They would go on "collecting tours" through the South, recording old songs, which became a part of the American Folk-Song Archive in the Library of Congress. Later, Lomax traveled to Great Britain, Italy, and Spain, and recorded the folk music of these countries as well. He was a pioneer in his field.

The iron handles on these boards were used as noisemakers for accompanying early European folk music.

The cog rattle was first used in medieval Europe as a worship instrument.

tainment, meant for enjoying by the fire, for dancing, for raising the spirit, or for telling a story. Folk music is typically sung or performed by ordinary people for their own enjoyment or the enjoyment of others. (If you are familiar with the "Little House" series, you may remember that Laura Ingalls Wilder's family gathered

Many adolescents enjoy playing old folk music on modern guitars.

around the cook stove on a cold winter nights while Pa played his fiddle.)

Folk music is often but not always old. Nobody really knows how far back any particular song goes—100, 200, 2,000, or more years. Over time, a song composed by an individual is added to, subtracted from, and adapted freely by others. Words and tunes can change just as language does over time. The tune may go back hundreds of years but the latest verse may be a week old. Many tunes are lost forever, but a few become part of a great collective songbook in the minds of a people.

The origins of most folk songs are lost in the distant past. Their modern form may be nearly identical to the original or almost unrecognizable. They resonate with and reflect their culture and historical setting. As time and history progress, they will fade into obscurity or adapt to new conditions.

Sometimes folk music is described as a music that is characteristic of a particular group of people—a tribe, religion, language, nationality, or culture. This description could be used in reference to jazz, rock, and practically all music. These musical styles originated in folk music. Even classical composers (like Anton Dvorak and Aaron Copeland) have borrowed freely from folk melodies.

In North America, the definition of folk music is further blurred by a relatively recent form of music we could call "folk-style music," a style of music that became very popular in the mid-20th century. Folk artists performed old folk music, but they also wrote new "folk-style" music, which means we now have new "folk" songs. We know the composers; the songs are professionally arranged, copyrighted, and performed; and so this music is not truly folk music, according to a folklorist's definition. Most of this music,

even though it is written down and recorded, will fade and disappear. But because of the traditional styles, some of the music will endure. Over time it will become a part of the culture. People will add their own words to the tunes, and they will become a part of us—true folk music.

The old songs are heard less and less, crowded out by almost limitless polished and professional music on radio and television. The rough raspy voice doesn't compete well with the trained voice. The cigar box banjo can't be heard above the modern blue-

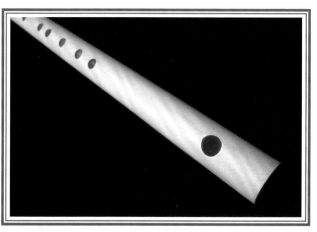

grass banjo or the electric guitar. My kids don't know the songs we sang as kids. The sheer volume of new musicians is crowding out folk music. Today, rather than the old reed parlor organ, a full orchestral score provided by tape or CD accompanies the wobbly amateur voices of backwoods churches.

Rattles were some of the simplest folk instruments and they came in all shapes and sizes.

But the foundation of modern music is the folk music of the past. The rhythms, scales, melodies, and harmonies of modern musical styles, R&B, Rock, Country, and Southern Gospel all have ancient roots, roots that are sunk deep in the soil of folklore.

String instruments can be used for classical music—or for folk music.

TWO

Strings and Things
Folk Instruments

Although the banjo originated in Africa, today it is considered to be a North American folk instrument.

FOLK INSTRUMENTS are as varied as the music that comes out of them. In the early days of folk instruments, many different makers experimented with different materials and shapes. Over time, some forms were discovered to work better than others. Other makers accepted those particular forms. Eventually, an instrument would assume a "classic" form, and subsequent changes would be pretty minor—until the instrument was needed for a different style of music and the whole process of change began again. This can be seen in the violin of the 18th century, the classic guitar of the mid 19th, and the five-string banjo of the late 19th. Still the tinkering goes on. The "classic" six-string guitar now has hundreds of relatives in acoustic and electric styles.

Instrumental folk music reflects the state of development of the instruments of the times. Most of our music was created after the violin assumed its present form, so folk musicians play the same instrument today as 150 years ago. The banjo is different; 150 years ago you could still find fretless gourd banjos.

The progression to a classic form also shows up in the tuning of an instrument. Older established instruments like the violin or mandolin were tuned in a standard way: GDAE (lowest pitch to highest pitch). Techniques of retuning the fiddle still linger in older Southern tradition as well as in French Canada. Guitars are usually tuned in the standard EADGBE, though blues musicians invented several important retunings of the guitar. Standard modern banjo players use gDGBD or gCGBD. Old-time folk players used the same tunings but also a wide variety of other

A "'tater bug" mandolin.

tunings, such as gCGCD, gDGCD, aEADE, or aDAC#E. (The small letter represents the short drone string on the five-string banjo.) Different tunings give a different sound or "flavor" to the music: sad, lonely, bright, or happy.

Some instruments are popular in widely differing styles of music. They develop more than one classic form. There are, for example, three main shapes for mandolins. The 'tater bug looks like a miniature lute with the body shaped like half of a pear. The frying pan mandolin looks like a large frying pan with a hole in the lid. The F5 model, popular in modern bluegrass, looks vaguely like a fat violin.

Most folk instruments are either homemade or inexpensive factory-built models. Homemade instruments come in an infinite variety of sounds and shapes and can be as simple as a cigar box fiddle or banjo, or complex instruments requiring woodworking skill, such as dulcimers, hammered dulcimers, guitars, and violins. Inexpensive factory instruments are much more uniform and include harmonicas, mandolins, concertinas and accordions, and guitars, banjos, and ukuleles.

Folk instruments are often played differently, usually by ear and imitation of a more accomplished player who also learned to play from others. The playing styles are passed down from one generation to the next. It is common to find both folk singers and instrumentalists who can't read a note of music.

BANJO

Considered the one most uniquely American instrument, the banjo really originated in Africa. Similar to instruments still found in the Savannah regions of West Africa today, early descriptions of a banjo-like instrument are described as an instrument made from half a calabash (a large gourd) and covered with skin scraped like parchment, with a rather long neck. Four strings of silk or dried bird gut were raised on a bridge above the skin. It was played by plucking and beating on the strings.

African American slaves played early American banjos. These instruments were made from half a gourd with a wooden neck. The number of strings varied, but they were generally made with a gourd over which some sort of skin was stretched. Joe Sweeney, a Southern **minstrel** player claimed to have invented the fifth string. He may have added an extra melodic string, but the short drone-string attached part way up the neck was already in use among African American banjoists and was an African contribution. The repeated striking of the high-pitched string gives the banjo a familiar ringing sound. By the mid-1800s, banjo makers started using round cheese box hoops, giving the banjo the familiar "frying pan" shape.

A banjolin is a combination of a banjo and a mandolin.

FIDDLE

Violins, in contrast to banjos, reached their classic form in the 1700s. While folk instrument makers used materials at hand—local curly maple lumber for backs and sides and necks, spruce for the soundboard, and willow for the lining—violins looked very much like they have for hundreds of years.

The violin is the one instrument common to nearly all types of folk music in North America, since it was the instrument available when waves of immigrants crossed the ocean. Small and lightweight, it fit easily onto a crowded ship, and as the population of the New World grew, fiddle makers copied the old instruments, using native woods.

In spite of the uniformity of the instruments, playing styles vary widely depending on the region in which they are played. While classical violinists tuck the violin under their chin, many fiddlers tuck it against their armpit or chest. A fiddler from one area may "saw" out a tune with the bow; another will use long smooth strokes for the same tune.

GUITAR

The guitar came to America as a parlor instrument played mostly by young ladies in the 19th century, but folk musicians quickly adopted it to accompany instrumental tunes at dances and jams. In the South, both white and black musicians devised astonishing new ways to play the guitar, creating new folk styles—including those amazing blues finger-picking and slide-guitar styles—that revolutionized both folk music and American popular music.

WOODCHUCK BANJO

Folk instruments, like the music played on them, are products of the materials of the culture from which they come. Folk banjos have been made from gourds and later cigar boxes, cans, or wooden hoops. Skin heads came from whatever was handy: goat, cat, deer, woodchuck. When I was young, I decided to experience firsthand this utilitarian folk music tradition.

One day in late fall on my half-mile walk home from school, I noticed a dead woodchuck wedged in a cleft of a hollow chestnut stump beside the path. Whether it had trapped itself and died a cruel death, or some prankster stuffed a dead chuck in the stump to leer at passersby I do not know, but an audacious plan popped into my head. There might be music in that dead woodchuck.

I didn't come from a family of hunters and had never skinned anything, but I consulted a library book, then sneaked the skin home (my mother would not have been delighted by my find), peeled the skin off with my jackknife, and coated the fur with a paste made from wood ashes. After a few days, the fur slipped right off, just like the library book said it would. With garage-sale hand tools, I whittled a banjo neck out of a piece of maple chair, boiled a slat of gum wood in a rain gutter, and bent it around a pail for a hoop. I copied the fret placements from a guitar and whittled wooden tuning pegs out of walnut. I stretched the rawhide skin over a smaller hoop and tacked it inside the bigger hoop. The rawhide dried and shrank up tight. After gluing and screwing everything together, I had a primitive banjo with a deep resonant kerplunkity sound. I learned to strum and pick out simple songs on it.

When I left home, Mom hung it in the living room as a decoration, and even 30 years later she won't give it back. I have built several banjos since with Mylar heads, curly maple, and fancy tuning machines. None sounds quite like that woodchuck banjo.

THE YOUNG MAN WHO WOULDN'T HOE CORN

(a good banjo folk song)

I'll sing you a song and it's not very long,
It's about a young man who wouldn't hoe corn.
The reason why I cannot tell,
This young man was always well.

He planted his corn on June the last,
By July it was up to his eye.
In September there came a frost,
And all this young man's corn was lost.

He took his hoe to the field at last,
And the weeds and the grass was up to his chin.
The jimson weeds they grew so high,
It made this young man for to sigh.

Now his courtship had just begun,
Saying, "Young man, have you hoed your corn?"
"I've tried, I've tried, I've tried in vain,
But I don't believe I'll raise one grain."

"How can you come to me to wed,
Why you can't raise your own corn bread.
Single I am and will remain,
A lazy man I won't maintain.

"You go down and propose to the widder,
And I hope to the dickens that you don't get her."
She gave him the mitten sure as you're born,
And all because he wouldn't hoe corn.

Now his courtship was at an end,
On his way he then began,
Saying, "Kind miss, I'll have another girl,
If I have to ramble the whole wide world."

PIANO AND ORGAN

The organ and piano also began their American life in the 19th century as church and parlor instruments. But it was not long before they were adopted and adapted by folk musicians. They were used to accompany fiddle tunes and to play at dances, and in places like Nova Scotia the piano players often play the tunes right along with the fiddler. Meanwhile, grassroots churches began devising new styles for organ and piano in gospel music.

ACCORDION

The accordion came from Germany in the 19th century and was quickly adopted in many folk traditions in America, from German American orchestras to Cajun music in Louisiana, *conjunto* Spanish music in the Southwest, polka bands in the Midwest, and many other ethnic traditions like Irish or Russian music in the big cities of North America. The accordion family ranges from little button concertinas to big multiple-keyboard accordions.

HARMONICA

The harmonica is also a German import that quickly took hold as a New-World favorite, whether for quiet solo playing like the cowboy's serenade or for lively dance music.

HAMMERED DULCIMER

The hammered dulcimer is an instrument found here and there throughout the New World. It has tiers of strings strung across a bridge on top of a wooden resonating chamber shaped like a rectangle or a trapezoid. The player beats on the open strings with two wooden hammers. A similar instrument from Central Europe is called the cymbalum. It is actually the ancestor of the piano, which mechanizes the action of the hammered dulcimer.

STRUMMED DULCIMER

This beautiful shy little instrument is common in the Appalachian Mountains and mostly unknown elsewhere. It is usually played on the lap. The three or four strings are strummed with a pick or quill. One or two are fretted to play the melody, while the others are "drone" strings and play the same note, which gives the interment a sound reminiscent of bagpipes. Dulcimers have no real standard shape. They can be teardrop shaped, hourglass, oval, or just box shaped.

SCALES AND MODES

Much of the flavor of folk music comes from the notes used. Look at piano keys. The white keys have an odd pattern of black keys squeezed between them. Two, then three, all the way up. Try playing all black keys. You get an almost eerie sound, and any combination of notes will make a nice sounding chord. The black keys give you a pentatonic (five-note) scale. This scale is common in Native American and Asian music.

Now on the white keys, start at middle C and play all the way up to the next C. This combination of half notes and whole notes is one of the most common modes. Now start at D and play up an octave. This is the same key of C but a different mode. It sounds, well, gloomy; it is good for sad sounding music. Start at E and play an octave; you get another "gloomy" scale. In fact, most modes are gloomy. That's probably why there is so much sad music in the world. Actually, many cultures use these **minor** modes for happy music. It's all in the way you hear it.

The modern version of this early European stringed instrument is the Portuguese guitarra.

THREE

Echoes from the
Old World
European Roots

The balalaika was brought to North America by Russian immigrants.

ALL OF EASTERN and Western Europe share a common musical heritage. It is impossible to know for sure, but we can guess that European music came from the music of the Roman Empire, the first really big superpower. At that time isolated tribes and cultures came into contact with each other as travel and trade became easier.

From the variety of modes (or scales) to how words are arranged in verses, the musical styles from Russia to Spain are remarkably similar. Perhaps the earliest roots of European music trace back to the early Christian church before the big Greek Orthodox–Roman Catholic **schism**. Today, people still listen to the early music: plainsong chants with simple modal melodies and minimal harmony. The music is pleasant to modern ears because it is recognizable as music. It is vaguely similar to modern music. Music from vastly different cultures, however, such as Australian aborigines or South American natives, may sound almost like pure noise to a person raised in the European culture.

While different styles from other regions have mixed in to a small extent, American folk songs as we know them today are mostly a hodgepodge of European songs. While we might expect Native Americans or Chinese immigrants might have influenced folk music, the quantity of these influences is practically nonexistent. It's probably not surprising. One the one hand, Native American music was so foreign to European ears, it sounded like noise (kind of what your music sounds like to your parents). And the European immigrants couldn't understand the words to the Native Americans' music either. On the other hand, the Native

From the 16th through the 18th centuries, Europeans played much of their music on harpsichords. The instrument was not suited for ocean travel, though.

Americans were not too fond of the new kids on the block. Their music was special to them, even sacred.

Most of our folk music traces back to Europe. Music came across the ocean in waves of immigration, and like the immigrants themselves, it did not blend quickly into the music of the land. The early Dutch settlers did not mingle much with the newly arrived English. The Germans arrived in multiple waves interspersed by the Irish and Italians, Jews, and Spaniards.

Even today, much ethnic music exists practically unchanged from its European roots. Polish and German polkas are unmistakably polkas. Songs that made the jump to North American folk music had to be attractive in some way. Most often a great tune was given English words. For example the Christmas carol "Silent Night" was written in the early 1800s in Germany. "Stille Nacht" was translated into English by John Young and has become a standard for Christmas carolers.

Most of American folk music comes from England, the land of our shared language. Everyone sang in "Olde Englande," and they brought their songs with them crammed into treacherous wooden boats to build a new life in the New World.

While we think of folk music as being transmitted from person to person, in fact folk music has been written down for over 500 years. In the early days of the printing press, popular tunes were printed on "broadsides." The term originally referred to anything printed on one side of a sheet of paper such as handbills or advertisements. For convenience, these were folded into "chapbooks" (buy-books). They were sold by "chapmen" who traveled from town to town, and collections of songs were known as "garlands." Chapbooks contained only the words with a note to sing the song to a popular tune. You'll still find many of these old tunes in church hymnals with the tune names listed in the index. These chapbooks were immensely popular up to the 19th century, before newspapers replaced them. Today we have sheet music or collections bound into books with not only words, but melody, accompaniment, and guitar chords.

Besides the broadsides, the other source of early folk music was the church. Henry Ainsworth, one of the Separatists to arrive at Plymouth Rock with the Pilgrims, took the psalms of the Bible and set them to music. Psalmbooks were popular in the colonies, when church singing was quite different from what it is today. No tapes with orchestral accompaniments and 200-voice choirs could be

A small guitar like this one might have been played by early immigrants from Italy.

Another early stringed instrument, called a colascione, *which was played in Italy in the 16th and 17th centuries.*

found anywhere. Instead, the minister would chant out a line of the psalm, and the congregation repeated the same line.

THE STRUCTURE OF EUROPEAN MUSIC

In Europe, poems tend to be grouped into sets of lines or stanza. For instance,

> *Mary had a little lamb.*
> *Its fleece was white as snow,*
> *and everywhere that Mary went,*
> *the lamb was sure to go.*

This familiar rhyme has four lines, and the four lines tell a complete thought. Compare this to a piece from a well-known Hebrew song:

> *The Lord is my shepherd.*
> *I shall not want.*
> *He makes me lie down in green pastures*
> *He leads me beside still waters*

He restores my soul
He leads me in the paths of righteousness for his name's sake. . . .

In this case, the thought progresses through the whole song.

In European music, each syllable of a word has its own special note. By contrast, African American singers tended to slur up and down the scale on the same syllable.

In Europe, narrative songs were common. These songs told a single story (ballads) or a long complicated story consisting of many events with a consistent theme (epics). While narrative songs occur in other regions of the world as well, they were less common than they were in Europe.

Love songs are more common in the European tradition than they were in other regions. These types are often sad yearning songs:

Alas my love, you do me wrong to cast me out so discourteously,
When I have done to you no wrong, delighting in your company.
("Greensleeves")

Sometimes they are songs about love and death:

I'm dreaming now of Hallie, dear Hallie, sweet Hallie. . . .
She's sleeping in the Valley. . . .
And the mockingbird is singing o'er her grave.

Distressingly common were horrible songs of murder and death. Themes included mothers killing their children, men killing their wives or girlfriends, robbers plundering and murdering travelers, pirates, and of course the final justice, the gallows. Europe was not a very happy place, judging from the predominant subject matter of the music. (Of course, judging from the movies, 21st-century North America isn't much better.)

In 1745, Scottish Prince Charles immigrated to North Carolina with a large number of his subjects. They brought with them this delightful ballad of poison, treachery, and love spurned:

"Where have you been all the day, Randall, my son?
Where have you been all the day, my pretty one?"
"I've been to my sweethearts, Mother,
I've been to my sweethearts, Mother."

chorus:
"Make my bed soon, for I'm sick to my heart,
and I fain would lie down."
"What have you been eating there, Randall, my son?
What have you been eating there, my pretty one?"
"Eels and eel broth, Mother,
Eels and eel broth, Mother."

chorus

"Were did she get them from, Randall, my son?
Where did she get them, my pretty one?"

An early European bass stringed instrument, called a lirone.

"From hedges and ditches, Mother,
From hedges and ditches, Mother."

chorus

"What was the color of their skins, Randall,
my son?
What was the color of their skins, my pretty
one?"
"Spickled and spackled, Mother,
Spickled and spackled, Mother."

chorus

"What will you leave your brother, Randall, my son?
What will you leave your brother, my pretty one?"
"My gold and silver, Mother,
My gold and silver, Mother."

chorus

"What will you leave your sweetheart, Randall, my son?
What will you leave your sweetheart, my pretty one?"
"A rope to hang her, Mother,
A rope to hang her, Mother."

Perhaps things weren't as wretched as they seemed!

Songs were also used to disseminate news. News items were printed in verse to fit to a well-known tune. Just as today, bad news sold better than good news. While discouraged by authorities, these broadsides were popular sale items. As early as ten years after the landing of the Pilgrims in New England, the

The tambourine goes back to the Middle Ages. The Crusaders brought it to Europe from the East.

presses were churning out broadsides. Benjamin Franklin wrote songs about recent events when he was only nine years old. His older brother printed them, and young Ben hawked them on street corners.

Songs about current events sold better than old ballads. In the absence of tune composers, writers of broadsides borrowed old tunes for new words. Over time, the old words were forgotten. But the tunes lingered. In fact, many are still being sung today.

The banjo came to the New World from Africa.

FOUR

North America's African Heritage
The Folk Music of African Americans

One of the most primitive of stringed instrument was simply a strung bow. Pressure from the player's thumb on the string altered the pitch.

THE FOLLOWING story occurs in various forms in different areas. It illustrates the power of music.

ONCE there was a little boy. As he wandered down the dusty road he sang a song:

> *Going down to Grandma's pea patch*
> *To get my little flute-tu*
> *To play for little sister*
> *And flute-tu for Aunt Lu.*

It was a sad little song, the way he sang it. It made you reach for your handkerchief and wipe your eyes. Even the clouds up in the sunny sky drizzled when they heard it.

By and by he met a fox.

"Where you going, son?" the fox asked. He was always hungry and wondered how that boy would taste with onions and carrots.

"Going down to Grandma's pea patch."

"What for?"

"To find my little flute-tu to play for little sister and Aunt Lu."

"Can you sing it?" the fox asked.

The little boy sang sadder than he ever sang before:

> *Going down to Grandma's pea patch*
> *To get my little flute-tu*
> *To play for little sister*
> *And flute-tu for Aunt Lu.*

Today's rock musicians, with their sound studios and synthesizers, still owe their musical heritage to African Americans.

Before long the fox pulled a hanky out of his back pocket and wiped his eyes. Above, the puffy little clouds in the sky commenced to drizzle, and the trees flipped their leaves upside down and rustled sadly.

"That there is a mighty sad song," the fox sniffed. Not wanting the boy to see him cry, he ran off into the woods.

The little boy walked on down the road singing sadly to himself. By and by he met a moss-backed snapping turtle. He was the biggest, meanest, and oldest turtle in those parts, pretty near 175 years old if he was a day. "Where you going, son?" the turtle asked. He hadn't eaten since he'd caught an eel three days ago, and he wondered how a little boy would taste with clam sauce.

"Going down to Grandma's pea patch."

"What for?"

"To find my little flute-tu to play for little sister and Aunt Lu."

"Can you sing it?" the turtle asked.

The little boy sang even sadder than he sang for the fox:

> *Going down to Grandma's pea patch*
> *To get my little flute-tu*
> *To play for little sister*
> *And flute-tu for Aunt Lu.*

The big old snapper rubbed and poked at his eyes with his claws. Above, the puffy little clouds commenced to drizzle, and the trees flipped their leaves upside down and rustled sadly. Even the rocks half buried in the ground by the road were wet with stony tears.

"That's a mighty sad song," the turtle sobbed. He clumped off into the swamp because he didn't want the boy to see him cry.

The little boy continued on down the road singing sadly to himself. Then he came around a bend and stopped up short. There stood the devil himself, horns, pointy beard, and all.

"Where you going, son?" the devil oozed, all warm and friendly like he was the boy's best friend.

"Going down to Grandma's pea patch."

"What for?"

"To find my little flute-tu to play for little sister and Aunt Lu."

"Can you sing it?" the devil asked.

The little boy closed his eyes and poured all the sadness he could into the song:

> Going down to Grandma's pea patch
> To get my little flute-tu
> To play for little sister
> And flute-tu for Aunt Lu.

As the devil listened, he grew red with anger. Just before the boy finished, he threw a sack over the boy, tied it tight, and slung him

Drums were vital to African American music. During slavery, however, drums were often forbidden.

over his shoulder. He took the boy home and threw him into the cellar, locked the door, and headed back out to look for more souls.

The little boy knew he was in a real fix this time. To bolster his spirit, he sang his sad song. The moldy pumpkins and turnips left in the cellar from last winter wept, and the coal turned so wet it wouldn't burn later even for the devil.

The devil's wife heard the sad singing coming from the basement. "What are you singing, boy?" she asked him.

"I'm singing about going down to Grandma's pea patch."

"Let's hear you sing it, then."

"It's so stuffy down here. If you could just open that door a little more and let some fresh air down here, I could sing it a lot better."

The devil's wife opened the door a little more, and the boy started to sing the saddest he had ever sang in his life.

> *Going down to Grandma's pea patch*
> *To get my little flute-tu*
> *To play for little sister*
> *And flute-tu for Aunt Lu.*

Pretty soon the devil's wife was just crying her eyes out. She cried so hard she didn't see the boy slip out the door, run out of the house, and dash away just as fast as his legs could ever carry him. He ran all the way down to Grandma's pea patch and found his little flute-tu.

As this African American folktale illustrates, music has power—power even to free us from danger and captivity. Far from their homes, in a strange and hostile world where they had lost nearly everything, African American slaves used music to

A primitive drum made from a hollowed-out tree trunk.

hold on to their identity, their dignity, and their hope.

While European music has been put to paper for hundreds of years, for centuries African music was passed on only by word of mouth. In fact, African music does not actually fit into the European system of written music. Rhythms are too complex. Some beats are struck just off the main beat. African musical scales, like European folk music scales, are different from the scales found in European art music (classical music). African and African American music uses vocal effects such as quavering, singing some notes "just off key" to European ears, and sliding from note to note.

Primitive instruments still found in West Africa vaguely resemble European instruments, particularly instruments that play somewhat like a fiddle, the *kukuma* and *goge*, and the primitive banjo, a stringed instrument remotely similar to the guitar.

Drums were discouraged and even forbidden in America for slaves, since these instruments had purposes other than entertainment. Slaves used them for communication and could signal revolts with their beat.

The slaves' life was far from pleasant. Music was often their

When no formal musical instruments are available, stones, bones, and shells work to create a beat. Children have always practiced this primitive music, and the early African Americans did as well.

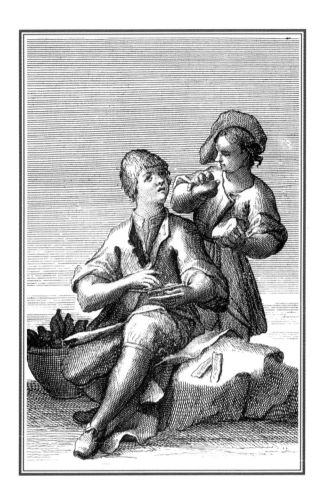

primary pleasure. Slave owners encouraged music, and even provided instruments for the slaves, probably to increase morale and productivity. African Americans took naturally to European instruments, freely adapting their own musical styles to the instruments.

During the period of slavery, contact between the races was common. European and African musicians freely intermingled, and musical styles influenced each other. Slave musicians were often called upon to entertain whites, and they could play jigs and reels as well as any white musician. Some church denominations such as the Methodists and Baptists believed in the equality of races; these believers worshipped and sang together.

SPIRITUALS

A large proportion of African American music was spiritual in nature. Of course much of white music was spiritual also, but for whites, religious and secular music was separated, while for the African Americans, spirituals shaped their everyday lives. Historical references indicate that white people noticed that the slaves seemed to be always singing hymns.

Those who study the origin of various songs note the similarity between the African American spirituals and white hymns compared to music found on the coast of West Africa. Depending on their point of view, **musicologists** will argue either that most African American music was influenced by European music or vice versa. It's probably impossible to ever know for sure. The scale of West African songs are similar to the scale and modes of African American spiritual music—and some European songs may well have fit these scales and modes, so that they were surely freely borrowed and changed to fit the African style.

MUSICAL STRUCTURE

Call-and-Response Chant

A leader calls out a phrase and the other singers answer back, often before the leader has finished the phrase. Today the call-and-response style is still common, both in Africa and in North America. For instance, I remember back when I was in Boy Scouts singing call-and-response songs that were surely a direct descendant of old African music, for all that they were semi-Christianized. I'll bet you've sung this song too.

> Oh you can't get to Heaven
> *(Oh you can't get to Heaven)*
> On roller skates

(On roller skates.)
'Cause you'll roll right past
('Cause you'll roll right past)
Those pearly gates
(Those pearly gates.)

I recall another verse that can surely be traced to the very dawn
of history:

Oh you can't get to Heaven
(Oh you can't get to Heaven)
On Superman
(On Superman)
'Cause the Lord He is
('Cause the Lord He is)
A Batman fan. . . .

Shouts

Shouts or ring shouts are a type of singing and dancing not often
found in European cultures. A circle of people moves single file
in a ring, accompanied by stamping and heel clicking. The song
is repetitive and can last for hours. The tempo or speed increases
gradually, and the excitement or emotional level builds over
time. The same phrase is repeated over and over until the partic-
ipants seem to enter an altered state of consciousness (often re-
garded as "possession by the Holy Spirit"). While this type of
music took on a "Christian" form, it appears to be similar to
African worship practices. It frightened slave owners, who tried
to discourage it.

Surges

Another form of spiritual song that appears in America is sung in slow, long phrases of highly decorated melody, sometimes called the "surge" style. It is similar to some European singing styles, but with added "Africanizations" such as off-the-beat timing and sliding notes. This style was also common in 17th-century Europe and 18th-century North America, leading some musicologists to believe it was a musical form copied by African Americans and developed to fit their singing style.

AFRICAN AMERICAN SECULAR MUSIC

The best known of African American musical **genres** is now known as the "blues." Some of the richest, profoundest, yet simplest music to resonate across cultures comes out of pain, poverty, sadness, and loneliness.

The origin of the blues is not known, although it is supposed that it began with the simple "holler," a single phrase that usually expressed sadness or loneliness:

A typical blues stanza is complete in 12 bars or measures; the first line is repeated one more time, and the final phrase completes the thought of the verse. Blues are suitable for a single singer alone or for simple accompaniment or small groups.

My woman done left me.
Feelin' awful bad. . .

If you were working in the middle of a field all alone from morning to night (with no boom box), you would probably holler too. You wouldn't just shout the words, though. As you worked, the rhythm of your body would make your words sound more like a chant. Another worker in another part of the field, who is as bored and lonely as you are, might answer back:

His woman done left him.
He's feelin' awful bad. . .

Musicologists wish someone was hiding at the edge of the field with a primitive tape recorder. Many of these academics are convinced that all musical genres started with simple, single lines, then evolved to become more complex. If we accept that as true, a hundred years later, this simple holler might have the third line added:

My woman done left me.
Feelin' awful bad. . .
Yeah, my woman's found another man
Makes me kinda sad.

The utter simplicity of the blues' form gives it its power. The lyrics are simple and repetitive, and the musical framework simple and loose. It is easy to improvise or make up words and tunes as you sing.

The blues as we recognize them today formed by the beginning of the 20th century. By the 1920s, record companies were recording blues musicians. Blues music earlier than this was not written down, so no one really knows how it developed or what exactly it sounded like. Early singers created their own songs or changed existing songs freely.

The powerful, sorrowful, soulful blues sound comes partly from the "blues scale." If you like to fool around with a musical instrument and make satisfying noises, try memorizing these notes and play them in various combinations. This is the blues scale in C. Of course you are free to mix other notes when improvising, but these will give you a nice bluesy sound:

Blues scale: C D Eb E F F# G A Bb C

Once you get the notes down, remember the rhythm is different in blues. **Syncopation** is important. Instead of counting your eighth notes as your piano teacher, Miss Bach, makes you practice, think of the eighth notes more as triplets with the center note missing. (Hopefully, you get the idea.) Now imagine your pet turtle just died and your mom flushed it down the toilet before you came home from school. Play your heart out.

John and Alan Lomax, in their book Our Singing Country, *described the "hollering songs" that were the blues' roots:*

Usually [hollering songs] consist of a two-line stanza in which the singer repeats the first verse two or three times and the last verse once—the whole introduced and followed by long drawn-out moaning or "yodeling" or shouts in the tempo and mood of the tune he was singing. They are sung with an open throat—shouted, howled, groaned, or moaned in such fashion that they fill a stretch of country and satisfy the wild and lonely and brooding spirit of the worker. The holler is a musical platform from which the singer can freely state his individual woes, satirize his enemies, and talk about his woman.

. . . The melodies are so free that it is impossible to give an adequate picture of them even by transcribing entire songs in musical notation. In mood they run the gamut of the worker's emotional life: his loves and sorrows, his hope and despair, his weariness, his resentment.

"Oo—oo—oo—oo—uh!
If I feels tomorrow like I feels today
Take a long freight train wid a red caboose
to carry my blues away."

An old blues "holler" collected by Alan and John Lomax:

Mamma, Mamma, make me a garment,
And make it long, white, and narrow.

Mamma, Mamma, look on my pillow
And you will find some money.

Get along, boys, and gather 'round me,
Come pay my fine, come and get me.

My true love died the other day,
I believe I'll die tomorrow.

Musicologists argue over how much European music influenced African or vice versa, but it may be more accurate to look at the union of cultures as producing a new music with hybrid vigor; in other words, music that is richer and better than either parent. In any case, today's styles of popular North American music—from the blues to jazz to rock'n'roll—all are rooted in African American music. The distinct character of North America's music owes an inestimable debt to that immense continent across the Atlantic.

Leadbelly was a former African American convict who became famous as a folksinger, thanks to the help of the Lomaxes. Leadbelly had this to say about the blues:

You never heard a white man could sing the blues in your life, have you? You know the reason why? They don't have them. Blue was composed up by the Negro people when they was under slavery. They was worried.

When you lie down at night sometime, it ain't too hot and it ain't too cold, but you turning from side to side. What's the matter? Blues got you. When you get up in the morning, the blues is walkin' 'round your bed. . . . What's the matter with you? The blues got you.

Have you ever heard the words of this old blues song from the South? The rock band the Animals turned it into a popular song in the 1960s, but it was around long before that.

There is a house down in New Orleans
they call the Rising Sun.
And it's been the ruin of many poor girl,
and me, oh God, I'm one.

My mother was a tailor,
she sewed these new blue jeans.
My sweetheart was a gambler, lord,
down in New Orleans.

Now the only thing a gambler needs
is a suitcase and a trunk.
And the only time he's satisfied
is when he's all a-drunk.

He fills his glasses up to the brim
and he'll pass the cards around.
And the only pleasure he gets out of life
is rambling from town to town.

Oh tell my baby sister
not to do what I have done
but shun that house down in New Orleans
they call the Rising Sun.

The keys of an accordion (or melodeon) look like a piano. The accordion is an essential instrument for Cajun music.

FIVE

Cajun Spice
Music of the French Settlers
in Louisiana

Cajun musicians are good fiddlers.

SEVENTEENTH-CENTURY settlers left France and settled in Acadia, New France, now known as Nova Scotia (New Scotland) in Canada. In 1755, the British threw them out of New France and deported many to English colonies in what is now the southern United States. These areas, originally inhabited by Spanish settlers, welcomed the influx of more Catholics. The Acadians or 'Cadians (eventually shortened to Cajuns), as they called themselves, mingled with Native Americans and free African Americans. The big Mississippi brought contact with Hispanics and English—and the resulting music mix came to be known as Cajun music.

Like other forms of folk music, the Cajuns kept their old music, adapting elements from other cultures with which they came in contact. The music developed freely until the 1920s recording era, when companies put the music on records. The sound caught on; preserved, it became a standard form.

The primary instruments of Cajun music were the violin and later the accordion. Violins were well known to the French, who carried them over the ocean to the New World and on into the South. Difficult to play but versatile, the violin was well suited to French music.

The accordion came to Louisiana with an influx of German immigrants in the late 1890s. This instrument's ease of playing, indestructibility, and volume fit well with folk music, and by the turn of the century the fiddle faced major competition. By the 1920s, the accordion overtook the fiddle in popularity. Its novelty and simple brashness overcame the more versatile and traditional fiddle.

FREE REEDS

Perhaps the largest impact on folk music during the last 150 years comes from something that was not appreciated and was even scorned by serious musicians: the humble metal free reed. The principle was based on Asian instruments, particularly the sheng.

The sheng, also known as an Eastern mouth organ, was invented in China in 3000 BC. It was made of a series of bamboo pipes attached to each other in a semicircle and fitted with copper reeds. All the tubes fit into one mouthpiece. The ends of the bamboo tubes were covered by the fingers, and by blowing and inhaling into the mouthpiece and covering or uncovering various holes, it was possible to play both melodies and chords. The sheng played a five-note or pentatonic scale (similar to playing all the black keys on a piano). Today in Eastern countries many variations of the sheng can be found. In the 17th and 18th centuries, travelers brought mouth organs to Europe.

In the late 1700s, there was some experimentation with the copper reeds in pipe organs. The early results didn't catch on, and organ builders stopped using them. But in 1821, Christian Buschmann, a German clockmaker, built the first known harmonica-like instrument, called an "aura." It was used as a device for tuning other instruments rather than for making music. By 1827 another German clockmaker, Christian Messner, started manufacturing instruments based on Buschmann's aura.

Two years later, Cyrill Demian acquired the "rights" to manufacture the "akkordion," an instrument similar to the harmonica. Others copied it but had to change the name to avoid lawsuits. They called it the "handharmonika." Eventually the two terms entered the English language as accordion and harmonica.

The "free reed" instruments proved immensely popular and new instruments were developed. Unlike natural reeds made of plants, metal reeds are virtually indestructible, inexpensive to make, and never go out of tune, all perfect qualities for instruments that can be carried across country in wagons or on horseback by poor people without the technical knowledge required to maintain fussier instruments.

When we think of families of instruments such as woodwinds, brass instruments, or percussion, the metal free reed family is usually overlooked. It contains instruments from small harmonicas to concertinas, melodeons, and accordions. The free reed, once spurned by the pipe organ industry, became a staple in inexpensive parlor organs for homes and small churches across America.

While it's possible to play several keys and different modes on an accordion, not all notes are available. An accordion with a C tuning plays all seven notes in C, six notes in G and F, five notes in D and B-sharp, down to G-sharp, where the best you can do is drone one of two notes.

The Cajun accordion first developed in the early 1800s in Germany. Sometimes called a "squeeze box," the instrument had the advantage in an era before electric amplification: it was loud enough to be heard in crowded dance halls. What you probably think of as an accordion is strictly speaking a "melodeon," an instrument that plays two different notes on each button, depending on whether the bellows are squeezed or pulled, similar to inhaling and exhaling on the harmonica. Like the harmonica, if you are not careful you can run out of breath (or air) in the middle of a song. An accordion with a piano-style keyboard plays all notes regardless of whether the bellows are pushed or pulled.

The Cajun accordion is a **diatonic** instrument, using eight notes of a standard **major** or minor scale. The right hand usually has ten buttons for playing the scale. The left hand has a handgrip with two buttons for two bass notes and two chords, which must be played while working the bellows against the right hand. The thumb holds a hole closed. It is opened when air is needed quickly either to fill or empty the bellows.

During World War II, German accordions were hard to get, however. At the same time, the discovery of oil in the region brought outsiders to the area who were more accustomed to the violin and the popular music of the rest of the country, such as coun-

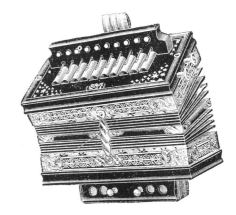

A lonesome desperate voice is singing of heartbreak and love. Singing in French. A fiddle adds plaintive drones and harmony. A boisterous accordion, all staccato attack and ornate rolls, provides lift and bounce. Beneath this trinity of voice, fiddle and accordion, a rhythm guitar and a great iron triangle jangle out a rude chanky-chank. The result is the quintessential sound of the South Louisiana prairies and bayous, Cajun music. . . .

The history of commercially recorded Cajun music, which goes back only to the late 1920s, can be read in part as the story of a long sibling rivalry. Big brother fiddle was with the Acadians in Canada, and its music was the base of the Cajun sound. Chromatic and fretless, it could easily handle all the subtleties of Cajun music, and was in many ways the primary instrument. Little brother accordion was newer on the scene and more limited in ability. Only seven different notes were available to the Cajun accordion, a single diatonic key. But what it lacked in subtlety, the accordion made up for in volume and sheer indestructibility. Four banks of reeds provided a huge sound that could be heard in a noisy house party, and its sturdy, boxy construction proved much less fragile than the fiddle's delicate, exposed fingerboard, strings and bridge. During much of Cajun music's recorded history, the two brothers have worked together beautifully and without complaint, but sometimes, as a result of broader social and historical patterns, one or the other has taken center stage. . . .

—Steve Winick

Zydeco is a currently popular type of French-language, African American music that emerged from a blend of Cajun, Caribbean, and African-American blues music traditions. Zydeco is faster and more syncopated than traditional Cajun music. It is a musical style uniquely native to Louisiana.

try-and-western bands. The fiddle returned to its former popularity.

After the war, young Cajun soldiers returned home with a feeling of *nostalgia* for what they considered the old traditional music. They liked the sound of the accordion, and once again the accordion dominated Cajun music.

Modern Cajun music recordings contain many "pop" elements, such as modern drums, electric guitar, trumpets, and saxophones. While traditionalists will complain, true folk music is always changing. It reflects the spirit and soul of the people it represents.

Bill Monroe is known as the Father of Bluegrass.

SIX

High and Lonesome
The Music of Appalachia

Lester Flatt and Earl Scruggs were early bluegrass musicians. If you've ever heard the theme song for The Beverly Hillbillies, *then you've heard their voices.*

I AM BLESSED to live at the very northern edge of the Appalachian Mountains. Just north of my home, the land flattens into big prosperous dairy farms and orchards. But only ten minutes to the south, the ancient hills rear up, and "gulches" or hollows open into the valleys. If I put my car into four-wheel drive and follow the dirt road up into one gulch overlooking the Canisteo Valley, I find a farm at the top that looks like one good rain could wash the gray barn and milk house into the valley.

"Hey, Pete," I'm often greeted. "We're having a hayride next week. Bring your banjo!"

On one such occasion, my family and I arrived just before dark. We climbed into the hay wagon lined with bales and loose hay to stave off the frosty autumn air. For the next two hours we sang. Old songs, new songs, television theme songs, and hymns. I heard songs I'd never heard before. The family had an enormous **repertoire**, perhaps because the wife came from a family of a dozen girls, and the husband's family had about as many boys; all those people were bound to collect songs.

The family scrapes their living off that crust of a hill, just as their ancestors did before them. And they still enjoy the old pastimes too. Their hayrides are a bit like going back in time, except the tractor has replaced the team of horses.

The Appalachian mountain range spans the east coast from Georgia to northern Pennsylvania (and continues on north into New England and the Canadian maritimes). The inhabitants, many of Scotch Irish descent, are known for their self-reliance and independence. Farming is marginal in the hilly terrain. The

 inhabitants of this region once supported themselves by logging and mining, both exceptionally hard and dangerous work. Traveling was difficult in the mountainous area. There was little time for pleasure.

Like their ancestors from Scotland and Ireland, the clan or extended family is a powerful force in Appalachian culture. According to one woman, "Its hard to meet new people, not enough time. We're always doing things with our family." Clannishness tends to isolate folks in remote areas, but during the 19th century, Apalachia was the crossroads of the United States, in the middle of the mainstream of American life. Its isolation was made more complete, however, by poor roads and no electricity or telephones in the early 20th century (and in some areas even in the present).

In this isolation, a distinct style of folk music could develop. Songs tended to stay in families and communities, without the cultural blending common in other parts of the country. Folk music changed from generation to generation, but not as much, and versions of many old songs can be traced back to similar songs in Europe.

One haunting song that caught on in the mining communities of Appalachia was originally a Victorian parlor song, "Don't Go Down in The Mine, Dad."

A miner was leaving his home for his work,
When he heard his little child scream;
He went to his bedside, his little white face,
"Oh, Daddy, I've had such a dream;
I dreamt that I saw the pit all afire,
And men struggled hard for their lives;
The scene it then changed, and the top of the mine
Was surrounded by sweethearts and wives."

CHORUS

"Don't go down in the mine, Dad,
Dreams very often come true;
Daddy, you know it would break my heart
If anything happened to you;
Just go and tell my dream to your mates,
And as true as the stars that shine,
Something is going to happen today,
Dear Daddy, don't go down the mine!"

The miner, a man with a heart good and kind,
Stood by the side of his son;
He said, "It's my living, I can't stay away,
For duty, my lad, must be done."
The little one look'd up, and sadly he said,
"Oh, please stay today with me, Dad!"
But as the brave miner went forth, to his work,
He heard this appeal from his lad:

CHORUS

Whilst waiting his turn with the mates to descend,
He could not banish his fears,
He return'd home again to his wife and his child,
Those words seem'd to ring through his ears,

"Don't Go Down in the Mine, Dad"

And, ere the day ended, the pit was on fire,
When a score of brave men lost their lives;
He thank'd God above for the dream his child had,
As once more the little one cries:

CHORUS

THE CARTER FAMILY

During the early years of the record industry, recording companies sent representatives up into the hills and hollows to find talent. They'd go into an area and put an ad into the paper looking for singers, fiddlers, and guitar pickers. Folks would trickle out of the mountains, sing and play, and if the music sounded promising, they could cut a record.

In 1927, Ralph Peer was looking for talent in Tennessee. There he met Alvin P. Carter, a salesman, and his wife Sara and Sara's cousin Maybelle, who was married to Alvin's brother. Maybelle sang tenor and played a distinctive

Folk music is kept alive in the hills of Appalachia.

The following is an Appalachian song that uses audience call and response; I learned it at one of those old-time hayrides. The singer sings the first phrase "One day I met. . ." and the audience repeats the same line. It's reminiscent of the African American work songs we discussed in chapter four.

SIPPING CIDER THROUGH A STRAW

One day I met, a handsome man
From sipping cider through a straw.
(audience repeats)
He asked me if I'd show him how
To sip some cider through a straw.
(audience repeats)
So cheek to cheek, and jaw to jaw,
We both sipped cider through a straw.
(audience repeats)
The straw did slip, our lips they met,
From sipping cider through a straw.
(audience repeats)
And now I've got a mother-in-law
From sipping cider through a straw.
(audience repeats)
And 14 kids, they call me "Ma,"
from sipping cider through a straw.
(audience repeats)
The moral of, the story is
To sip some cider through a straw
The moral of, the story is
To sip some cider, 'stead of Coke.
Dittle lote dote dote

In Appalachian tradition, singing was an important part of courting. Today most North American couples go out to dinner or to a movie, but once songs like the one that follows would have kept a couple occupied.

JENNIE JENKINS

Man: Will you wear white, O my dear, O my dear?
               Oh, will you wear white, Jennie Jenkins?

Woman: I won't wear white,
               For the color's too bright,
               I'll buy me a fol-de-roldy-tildy-toldy, seek-a-double, use-a-cause-a-roll-the-find-me.

Man: Roll, Jennie Jenkins, roll.
               Will you wear blue, O my dear, O my dear?
               Oh, will you wear blue, Jennie Jenkins?

Woman: I won't wear blue,
               For the color's too true,
               I'll buy me a fol-de-roldy-tildy-toldy, seek-a-double, use-a-cause-a-roll-the find-me.

Man: Will you wear red, O my dear, O my dear?
               Oh, will you wear red, Jennie Jenkins?

Woman: I won't wear red,
                It's the color of my head,
               I'll buy me a fol-de-roldy-tildy-toldy, seek-a-double, use-a-cause-a-roll-the-find-me.

Man: Will you wear black, O my dear, O my dear?
               Will you wear black, Jennie Jenkins?

Woman: Well, I won't wear black,
               It's the color of my back,
               I'll buy me a fol-de-roldy-tildy-toldy, seek-a-double, use-a-cause-a-roll-the-find-me.

Man: Will you wear purple, O my dear, O my dear?
            Will you wear purple, Jennie Jenkins?
Woman: No, I won't wear purple,
            It's the color of a turkle,
            I'll buy me a fol-de-roldy-tildy-toldy, seek-a-double, use-a-cause-a-roll-the-find-me.

Man: Will you wear green, O my dear, O my dear?
            Will you wear green, Jennie Jenkins?
Woman: No, I won't wear green,
            For it's a shame to be seen,
            I'll buy me a fol-de-roldy-tildy-toldy, seek-a-double, use-a-cause-a-roll-the-find-me.

lead guitar style. Sara sang the lead and played the autoharp, while Alvin added his deep bass voice. From the first audition until their final performance in 1941, the trio's smooth simple harmonies captivated people across the country. They recorded hundreds of songs in a large variety of styles. Other musicians imitated their instrumental style and harmonization, as the Carter family helped Appalachian folk music cross the line into mainstream North America.

BLUEGRASS

Today one of the closest direct descendents of old-time mountain music is the bluegrass style. Typically a bluegrass band has a fiddle player, a guitar, banjo, mandolin, and bass to accompany the singers. Bluegrass is considered old-time traditional music, but it is actually a form of modern music, professionally performed. This high-energy music, however, is still firmly rooted in old folk songs.

The name "bluegrass" comes from a popular group in the '40s, Bill Monroe and the Blue Grass Boys. Bill Monroe grew up in western Kentucky with his two older brothers, Charlie and Birch. Charlie played guitar; Birch played the fiddle; and Bill ended up playing the mandolin. When their parents died, the older boys headed north to the oil refineries near Chicago. Bill, still in his teens, went with them. They continued to play together, and when a group of square dancers started a touring company, the brothers played with the band.

By 1934, they were working regularly in South Carolina and found their popularity increasing. In 1935, the Victor Recording Company produced a record containing two of their songs; it turned out to be the biggest seller in the South up to that time.

Unfortunately, the more successful the brothers were, the less they got along. By 1938, after many years of playing together, they split, and Bill started his own band, the "Blue Grass Boys."

At that time, one of the biggest and most popular radio shows in the Southeast was the "Grand Ole Opry" on Nashville's radio station WSM. It was a mix of comedy, *vaudeville*, hymns, and traditional folk singing. When Bill Monroe and the Blue Grass Boys auditioned for the show, they were an immediate hit. Their powerful "high and lonesome" sound was different than anything

DON'T YA TELL PA

I love little Willie I do Ma Ma,
I love little Willie I do.
I love little Willie, but don't ya tell Pa!
Cause Pa wouldn't like it at all, Ma Ma.

He wrote me a letter, he did Ma Ma,
He wrote me a letter, he did.
He wrote me a letter but don't ya tell Pa!
'Cause Pa wouldn't like it at all, Ma Ma.

He told me he loved me, he did, Ma Ma,
He told me he loved me, he did.
He told me he loved me but don't ya tell Pa!
Cause Pa wouldn't like it at all, Ma Ma.

And now we are married, we are Ma Ma,
And now we are married, we are.
And now we are married but don't ya tell Pa!
'Cause Pa wouldn't like it at all, Ma Ma.

And now we are three, we are, Ma Ma,
And now we are three, we are.
And now we are three and you can tell Pa!
'Cause Pa can't do nothin' at all, Ma Ma.

Many songs sung in Appalachia were the same old ballads that were popular in England centuries ago. Ballads tell a story, like the song that follows:

THE MERMAID

As I went out one evening,
Far out of sight of the land,
There I saw a mermaid a-sitting on a rock
With a comb and a glass in her hand.

A-combing down her long yellow hair,
Her skin was like a lily so fair,
Her cheeks were like two roses and her eyes were like the stars,
And her voice was like the nightingale's air.

This little mermaid swum into the deep,
The winds began to blow,
The hail and the rain was so dark in the air,
We'll never see the land any more.

At last come down the captain of our ship,
With a plumb and a line in his hand;
He plumbed the sea to see how far it was
To a rock or else to the sand.

He plumbed her behind and he plumbed her before
And the ship kept turning around,
The captain cried out, "Our ship will be wrecked
When the needle swings around.

"Then throw out your loading as fast as you can,
The truth to you I will tell,
This night we all must start
To heaven or else to hell."

heard before. Over the following years, they became one of the most popular groups on the Grand Ole Opry. With their recordings, they helped the strains of Appalachian folk music spread across the country.

Bill hired Chubby Wise to play fiddle, Lester Flatt as vocalist and guitar player, and later Earl Scruggs on the banjo. By 1945, the Blue Grass Boys were the Beatles of their day. They began a new movement in traditional American music. Banjo became popular again, and mountain boys all the way down Appalachia's rocky spine dusted off their old five-strings so they could copy the Scruggs style.

By the early 1950s, radio pop music moved away from traditional music, but other bands still sprang up to play the "new traditional music," now for the first time called "bluegrass" music in honor of Bill Monroe and the Blue Grass Boys.

Hispanic street players play ancient melodies that go back to medieval Spain as well as long-ago Mexico.

SEVEN

An Old-World and New-World Hybrid
Hispanic Folk Music

Guitar music is an essential ingredient of Hispanic music.

LIKE THE FOLK music to the north, Southwestern folk music has many twisted and tangled roots. Unlike the eastward-reaching roots of the North, however, the musical roots of the Southwest reach down into Mexico. The European roots of Southwestern music are older and fainter than the English roots of Appalachian music, going back to 16th-century Spain. There is enough in common with folk music of the Northeast, however, to indicate a common background. For instance, Hispanic folk music is arranged in stanzas and the modes are the same. Still the music is distinctly different. More is borrowed from Native American music, since interracial marriages were more common between the Spanish colonists and Native Americans. The races mingled more in the Southwest, and they created a form of music that was unique to their culture. Hispanic folk music was the music of working people. Herding cattle over the long cattle drives or sheep herding, mining, and working on railroads all contributed to the music of North America's Southwest.

Perhaps the largest single barrier to the spreading of music across cultures is language. Still, where two cultures meet and intermingle, the music will cross any geographical borders. This process works both ways: Hispanic music styles have influenced the rest of North America's music, while Hispanic folk musicians have also picked up elements of North America's other music styles. For example, the well-known Hispanic folk song "Susanita" (Little Susan) is a version of *Oh Susanna* by Stephen Foster.

The broad spectrum of subject matter in Hispanic folk songs

Medieval Spaniards played a large guitar like this one.

illustrates the commonality of all human beings. True love, unfaithful love, murders, animals, accidents, war, alcohol abuse, hardship, love of God, love of family, sadness at the loss of parent or child—these are all themes reflected in the music of the Southwest.

Corridos or ballads are still popular in Mexico and the Southwest of the United States. They are similar to the Spanish **romances**, which were recited rather than sung. Narrative in form, the corrido tells a story. It is sung either as a solo, or with simple accompaniment, usually a guitar or a small band.

Alabados are hymns or passion ballads. Some come from Spain, others originated in Mexico. They are sung at holidays such as **Lent**, Christmas, and other religious holidays and funerals.

CONJUNTO

While the banjo took hold in the hills of Appalachian bluegrass music, the accordion became the fundamental instrument of *conjunto* (pronounced "con-hoonta," the Spanish word means "band"), an **ensemble** of traditional Mexican-American folk dance music. As was true of early Cajun music, these accordions were not the giant "Lawrence Welk"-style instruments but rather small simple button-style accordions.

In addition to the accordion, the *bajo sexto,* a small guitar, and the *tambora de rancho,* or ranch drum, accompanied the accordion in conjunto music. Other instruments popular in this form of Hispanic folk music are similar to those found in the rest of North America. The guitar, which comes originally from Spain, is one of the most

In the 17th century, the Spanish guitar spread to Italy, France, England—and the New World.

A 17th-century Spanish form of the violin.

popular. The violin often accompanied the guitar. The mandolin and harmonica sometimes filled out the ensemble.

Conjunto gained in popularity, especially after the 1920s when record companies started recording the music, and eventually it became the dominant music of the Hispanic working class. At that time, it lacked any established set of instruments, but by the end of the Second World War, the conjunto was a fully developed musical style. Modern trap drums replaced the tamboro de rancho, and the contrabass was added (and later the electric bass

LOS POLLITOS

(A Hispanic Folksong)

Los pollitos dicen:
"Pio pio pio"
Cuando tienen hambre
Cuando sienten frio.

La Mallina busca,
El maiz atrigo.
Para sus pollitos
Pio pio pio.

Translation:
The little chicks say
"Cheep cheep cheep,"
When they are hungry,
When they are cold

Mama hen searches
For dry corn
For her chicks
"Cheep, cheep cheep!"

guitar). The earlier conjunto music was almost completely instrumental, but now vocals were added as well.

Today conjunto music is either loved or hated by Hispanic North Americans. In either case, it remains an important form of music, one that is deeply rooted in the folk music of the past.

DATING OF MUSIC

So much music is passed around orally and changed with each singer, the process of determining the date is challenging. Many songs provide clues, which help musical sleuths in their investigation.

1. Since songs were a way of distributing news, many folk songs often start out with the date. The corrido or Hispanic ballad customarily began with the year and sometimes even the month and day of the event's occurrence. This establishes the earliest possible date. For instance, we know this poem was obviously written sometime after 1492:

    In fourteen hundred and ninety two
    Columbus sailed the ocean blue.

    Unlike the Columbus poem, ballads were usually written while the news was still fresh by pre-newspaper standards.

2. Old songs sometimes contain obsolete words or words that are no longer in common usage. These words can be compared with songs or literature of the same area and with a known date. In English we don't say, "Look at the kine grazing in the pasture." (Unless we just arrived in a time machine from Old England, we would use "cows" or "cattle.") The use of these words helps to date the song.

3. Old songs sometimes refer to inventions or modes of travel common to their era. In the case of "modern" inventions of the times, the standard words may not even be in use. A 1907 reference to "a birdman perched on a hill north of town" sounds peculiar to modern ears. We would say a pilot landed an airplane on a hill north of town.

4. Older songs may refer to customs no longer practiced (for example, kings and nobility or duels).

5. The modal scale of a song may vary with the time and location.

6. Musical styles can indicate an era. For instance, a waltz or polka style establishes a relatively narrow time frame and location for the song.
7. Old newspapers sometimes published poetry that then became folk music because of its popularity. By reading old newspapers, it is possible to sometimes find an author and date for what has become a folk song.
8. Music can sometimes be traced back to its country of origin. In the northern United States and in Canada, the migration of people was from East to West. In the Southwest, the migration was north from Mexico, then from across the ocean. Sing a Mexican corrido in Spain, and you may find a similar song there is already a well-known folk song.

You can hear folk music being played in the parks of almost any North American city.

EIGHT

Revival
Folk Music in the
20th and 21st Centuries

Folk music can be enjoyed by anyone.

FOLK MUSIC changed with the beginning of the Industrial Revolution. Just as Julia Ward Howe rewrote the Battle Hymn to reflect her righteous indignation over slavery, people wrote new words to the old songs to reflect their living and working conditions.

The latter half of the 19th century was an era of big factories, big railroads, and big banks. Ordinary folks worked long hours at dangerous jobs for low pay. When conditions became intolerable, the workers formed labor unions. Collectively, they could bargain for better pay, safer conditions, and shorter workdays. The people gathered at union rallies, and they often wrote new words to the old songs to inspire, motivate, and unify the workers.

The big corporations fought back. There were deadly skirmishes, and people were killed. New songs arose about those heroes fallen in battle. The workers staged strikes and picketed and sang about the injustices.

With the rise of the new Socialist political movement, folk songs turned into songs of protest—against the Great War (World War I), against social injustice, and against the government itself. During the Great Depression, various forms of *socialism* were looking pretty good to the poor, hungry people who were without work.

The biggest change of all came with the invention of radio. In 1900 a singer could reach thousands of people at a rally. By 1925, the same singer could reach millions through radio. Through the 1930s and '40s, folk music became immensely popular, and many radio shows were devoted to it. The folk singers were no longer farmers and factory workers, but full-time musicians. Their music remained political and social in nature.

One of the most important popular groups during the 1940s was the Almanac Singers. Among the various members of the group, the two best known are Pete Seeger and Woody Guthrie, who is known as the father of the modern protest ballad.

WOODY GUTHRIE

Woody Guthrie was born Woodrow Wilson Guthrie on July 14, 1912 in Okemah, Oklahoma. His father was a cowboy; while Woody was still a boy, he experienced the loss of his older sister, the financial ruin of his family, and the institutionalization of his mother. The Great Depression began when he was 17, and by the time he was 19, the once booming town of Okemah went bust.

Woody headed for Texas. He married in 1933 to Mary Jennings, the sister of a musician friend, Matt Jennings, and he and the Jennings formed "The Corn Cob Trio." The Depression made living as a musician difficult, and in 1935 the Great Dust Storm swept across the plains. Now there was no

The Chinese tseng is an early form of the zither, a distant cousin of today's folk instruments.

work at all. Woody migrated across the country along with thousands of other "Okies" (people from Oklahoma) and unemployed factory workers from other states.

He ended up in California in 1937. The residents of California did not like the tramps and hobos taking up residence in their state, and Woody was forced to endure their scorn and suspicion; the experience helped him identify with the downtrodden and dispossessed. He found he liked traveling the country by hitchhiking and riding freight trains. His songs reflected his troubles, and others hit hard by the Depression could relate to his music.

In 1939, he moved to New York City, where he met other artists, writers, and musicians who shared his views. He wrote music and performed with the Almanac Singers and later the Weavers, a group which did much to popularize folk music during the 1940s and '50s.

He took to the road again, however, after tiring of the entertainment industry. During World War II he served in the Merchant Marines and the Army, but music remained the focus of his life. Over the course of his life he won many awards. Perhaps his best-known song is "This Land Is Your Land." He died in 1967 of Huntington's disease, the illness that had affected his mother.

THE 1950s TO THE PRESENT

By the 1950s, the memory of the Depression was fading into the postwar prosperity. The folk movement was well established as a protest movement. Now, as it was taken over by professional popular musicians, folk enthusiasts argued endlessly over what folk music really was. They categorized it as contemporary, traditional, old time, bluegrass, pop-folk, and international. Songs were "adapted and arranged" by some groups. In other words, they hired a professional musician to arrange the music to give it a more polished sound. Other groups reacted by performing "authentic" music exactly as they heard it from earlier folk musicians. The controversies went back to the question: What is folk music? It was hard to define.

The "new" folk revival started when the Kingston Trio sang "Tom Dooley" in 1958. This cheerful song was originally written in 1868 by a man who sat in jail waiting for his execution:

This time tomorrow,
Reckon where I'll be?
In some lonesome valley
A-hangin' on a white oak tree.

With that inspiring start, folk suddenly turned pop. New folk groups sprang up all over.

People were drawn to the new folk music for many reasons. Urban people and residents

The Kingston Trio began the modern revival of folk music.

An Asian instrument called the sarinda *may have been an early fiddle.*

of the new "suburbias" that sprawled around the large cities were attracted to the nostalgia of simpler times. It reminded them of life on the farm. The music contrasted with the brash brass of the big bands, the driving hyperventilation of the new rock'n'roll, and the sophistication of the modern crooners. In sharp contrast, a few folk musicians strummed acoustic instruments and sang simple harmony. College students were looking for different styles of music. Songs of protest appealed to young idealistic people looking for meaning in their life.

The new definition of folk included old folk music and new "folk-style" music. The new folk continued to protest the "establishment" and eventually the war in Vietnam. Like the old labor union songs earlier in the century, it galvanized and unified protestors. They became a powerful force for social change.

The new folk movement centered around cities and university campuses rather than up in the hills and down in the hollers of Appalachia, on the Mexican frontier, or in Louisiania bayous. Many folk musicians ended up in Greenwich Village in New York City.

The old protest singers were still around, including Pete Seeger. New musicians appeared; one of them was a Minnesotan named Robert Zimmerman, also known as Bob Dylan. Among his many songs, "Blowin' in the Wind" became one of the anthems of the civil rights movement. Bob Dylan, because of his song, was considered a civil rights leader.

The year 1965 marked a major shift in folk music. Bob Dylan bought an electric guitar and turned more toward rock music. Folk music was too commercial for the traditionalists. Its popularity seemed to fade with the '60s' protests and the Vietnam War. It continues to the present, however, in a less conspicuous way among local musicians and a few folk programs on public radio.

And true folk music, the ancient tunes and musical styles passed from generation to generation, will never die. Nourished by its deep roots in past traditions, it will continue to grow and evolve, delighting future generations.

FINDING YOUR OWN FOLK MUSIC

Folk music is all around you, but it may be drowned out by TV, radio, movies, video games, sports, and all the other activities of a busy world. Still, the new music is connected to the folk music of the past.

Ask your grandparents, your great aunts and uncles. Keep your eyes open for weird musical instruments tucked away in attics. Chances are someone will remember Aunt Beulah used to play that zither or Uncle Henry played that cornet in a marching band. Lulu may have fiddled for square dances before she mar-

ried Uncle Geezer back in the
'50s. Harmonicas hiding in
junk drawers are a dead give-
away that someone around the
place used to play them.

Folk players are often shy
about their talent, feeling it will
be compared to modern digi-
tally produced synthesized music. Showing appreciation and in-
terest, asking if they might teach you a song or two, can bring
amazing results. For instance, I recently called a woman for
words to an old song and left with three (the Appalachian folk
songs I included in chapter six). The rest of her repertoire is just
waiting to be mined.

Check the neighbors. "Mr. Wilson, did you ever play an instrument before you turned into a crotchety old man who yells at
me when my soccer ball lands in your flower bed?" (You might
want to work on your approach a bit.)

"Why . . . er . . . oh . . . huh?" may be all the response you get
at first.

But then Mrs. Wilson fills in. "George used to be in the glee
club in college. And he was a wonder on the ukulele. Remember
'By the Light of the Stars,' George?"

"Why yes, I played that the night I proposed, didn't I. Where
is that old ukulele, anyway. . .?"

Recently, I discovered a treasure trove of folk music I hadn't ex-
pected when I brought some harmonicas to a family reunion. I
fancy myself a pretty good "tooter" for an amateur; I can get people
stomping and hooting with a good accompanist on a guitar or piano. But my second cousin Herb picked up one of the harmonicas
and in a style I never heard played the most beautiful melody with
his tongue working the harmony in a way that sounded impossible.

Where once folk music could only be passed along by means of human mouths, modern technology has changed all that. The 33 rpm "long playing"(LP) record looks like a black plastic stone age CD, about ten inches in diameter. It holds up to 45 or 50 minutes of music. It replaced the prehistoric 78 rpm records that could hold at most six minutes of music. Both use a metal needle instead of a laser to transmit sound to an amplifier and then to speakers. A hip cat could lounge in his pad listening to the music of his choice for hours. Inexpensive record albums gave people the chance to listen to anything. The album cover became something of an art form.

With each technological advance in recording, the musical industry seemed to explode. First, 78s replaced the early wax cylinders. Stackable 45s replaced the 78s. Then came the 33-rpm LPs, eight-track tapes, cassettes, CDs, and DVDs. The choice of music continues to grow.

Libraries, Salvation Army stores, and thrift stores usually have old LP records for sale. While collectors snatch up a lot of them, you can still find extremely cheap folk music. Look for folksy looking pictures on the album cover. Record players are still around. Check closets and attics at your relatives' houses.

Go with a group to an adult care facility. (Church groups often do musical programs.) You may find the residents' brains have stored an amazing number of old songs, some on the edge of disappearing forever. You might learn one and maybe sing it at school in a talent show. Who knows, a talent scout might be sitting in the audience. He can't get that song out of his head. He looks you up and invites you to cut a CD in Nashville. It wins a Grammy or a Dove award. . . .

Well, you never know.

> *Ring, ring de banjo,*
> *I like that good ole song.*
> *Come along my true love!*
> *Oh why you been so long?*
> —Stephen Foster

Further Reading

American Folksongs. New York: Hal Leonard Publishing, 1999.

Doyle, Donnie. *Along Lot Seven Shore: Folksongs and Other Writings.* New York: Acorn Press, 2001.

Lomax, John A. *Our Singing Country: Folk Songs and Ballads.* Mineola, N.Y.: Dover, 2000.

Lomax, John A. and Alan Lomax. *American Ballads and Folk Songs.* Mineola, N.Y.: Dover, 1994.

McNeill, W.K. *Southern Mountain Folksongs: Traditional Folksongs from the Appalachians and the Ozarks.* New York: August House, 1993.

Sandburg, Carl and Garrison Keillor. *The American Songbook.* New York: Harvest Books, 1990.

Sieling, Peter. *Folk Songs.* Philadelphia: Mason Crest, 2003.

For More Information

American Folk Music
www.jdray.com

Folk Music
www.contemplator.com/folk.html
www.acronet.net/~robokopp/English.html

Folksong Lyrics
Home.t-online.de/home/pheld/texte1a.htm

Folksongs and Ballads of the Appalachians
www.netstrider.com

Song Lyrics for Kids
www.kididdles.com/mouseum/y004.html

Glossary

Abolitionist   A person who fought to end slavery.

Diatonic   Musical scales with five whole steps and two half steps.

Ensemble   A musical group of two or more parts that creates a single effect.

Genres   Styles or categories.

Lent   The 40 weekdays before Easter, traditionally a time of spiritual self-examination.

Major   A musical scale that has half steps between the third and fourth, and the seventh and eighth degrees.

Minor   A musical scale having half steps between the second and third, and the fifth and sixth degrees.

Minstrel   troupe of performers who typically gave a program of African American songs and jokes, often with their faces blackened.

Musicologists   People who study music as a field of research.

Nostalgia   A sentimental yearning for something that lies in the past.

Repertoire   A collection of musical pieces available for performance.

Romances   A medieval tale based on legend, chivalry, and adventure.

Schism   Split, division.

Socialism   A political system where the government owns and distributes property.

Suffrage   The right to vote.

Syncopation   Rhythm that stresses what would normally be the weak beat.

Vaudeville   Stage entertainment consisting of various acts (such as comedians, dancers, and singers).

Index

Biographies

Peter Sieling is the owner of Garreson Lumber and the author and publisher of two technical books: *Bee Hive Construction* and *Air Drying Lumber for Maximum Yield*. In addition, he writes for *Bee Culture Magazine*. He enjoys playing the keyboard, harmonica, and banjo. He resides with his wife and three children in upstate New York, where several pea fowls, a goose, approximately 500,000 honeybees, and assorted cats and dogs also keep him company.

Dr. Alan Jabbour is a folklorist who served as the founding director of the American Folklife Center at the Library of Congress from 1976 to 1999. Previously, he began the grant-giving program in folk arts at the National Endowment for the Arts (1974–76). A native of Jacksonville, Florida, he was trained at the University of Miami (B.A.) and Duke University (M.A., Ph.D.). A violinist from childhood on, he documented old-time fiddling in the Upper South in the 1960s and 1970s. A specialist in instrumental folk music, he is known as a fiddler himself, an art he acquired directly from elderly fiddlers in North Carolina, Virginia, and West Virginia. He has taught folklore and folk music at UCLA and the University of Maryland and has published widely in the field.